THE LAS VEGAS RAIDERS

BY ALICIA Z. KLEPEIS

EPIC

BELLWETHER MEDIA ★ MINNEAPOLIS, MN

EPIC BOOKS are no ordinary books. They burst with intense action, high-speed heroics, and shadows of the unknown. Are you ready for an Epic adventure?

This book is intended for educational use. Organization and franchise logos are trademarks of the National Football League (NFL). This is not an official book of the NFL. It is not approved by or connected with the NFL.

This edition first published in 2024 by Bellwether Media, Inc.

No part of this publication may be reproduced in whole or in part without written permission of the publisher. For information regarding permission, write to Bellwether Media, Inc., Attention: Permissions Department, 6012 Blue Circle Drive, Minnetonka, MN 55343.

Library of Congress Cataloging-in-Publication Data

Names: Klepeis, Alicia, 1971- author.
Title: The Las Vegas Raiders / by Alicia Z. Klepeis.
Description: Minneapolis, MN : Bellwether Media Inc., 2024. | Series: Epic: NFL team profiles | Includes bibliographical references and index. | Audience: Ages 7-12 | Audience: Grades 2-3 | Summary: "Engaging images accompany information about the Las Vegas Raiders. The combination of high-interest subject matter and light text is intended for students in grades 2 through 7"-- Provided by publisher.
Identifiers: LCCN 2023021984 (print) | LCCN 2023021985 (ebook) | ISBN 9798886874822 (library binding) | ISBN 9798886876703 (ebook)
Subjects: LCSH: Las Vegas Raiders (Football team)--Juvenile literature. | Football teams--Nevada--Las Vegas--Juvenile literature.
Classification: LCC GV956.L59 K54 2024 (print) | LCC GV956.L59 (ebook) | DDC 796.3326409793/135--dc23/eng/20230512
LC record available at https://lccn.loc.gov/2023021984
LC ebook record available at https://lccn.loc.gov/2023021985

Text copyright © 2024 by Bellwether Media, Inc. EPIC and associated logos are trademarks and/or registered trademarks of Bellwether Media, Inc.

Editor: Kieran Downs   Designer: Josh Brink

Printed in the United States of America, North Mankato, MN.

TABLE OF CONTENTS

AN OVERTIME WIN	4
THE HISTORY OF THE RAIDERS	6
THE RAIDERS TODAY	14
GAME DAY!	16
LAS VEGAS RAIDERS FACTS	20
GLOSSARY	22
TO LEARN MORE	23
INDEX	24

AN OVERTIME WIN

JOSH JACOBS

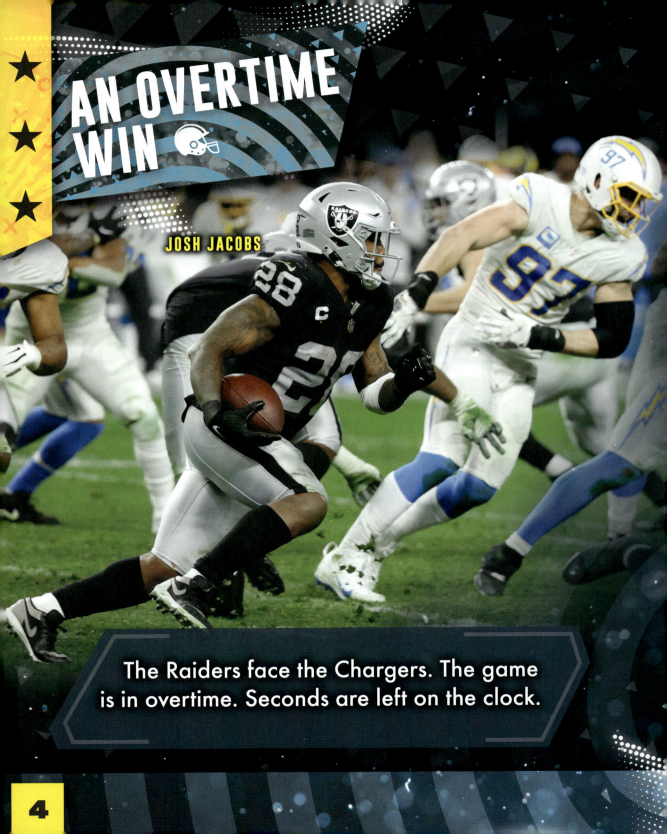

The Raiders face the Chargers. The game is in overtime. Seconds are left on the clock.

Running back Josh Jacobs runs for a **first down**. Daniel Carlson then kicks a 47-yard **field goal**. The Raiders win! They are heading to the 2021 **playoffs**!

DANIEL CARLSON

THE HISTORY OF THE RAIDERS

The Raiders began in Oakland, California, in 1960. They played in the American Football League (AFL) for ten seasons. The team struggled at first. Then, head coach Al Davis joined the team in 1963.

AL DAVIS

COACH TO OWNER

In 1966, Al Davis became a part owner of the Raiders. He took over completely in 1976.

1963 OAKLAND RAIDERS

The team began winning. They made it to the **Super Bowl** in 1968. But they lost.

A CHAMP OF A COACH

John Madden was the Raiders' head coach from 1969 through 1978. The team had a winning record in all ten seasons he was coach.

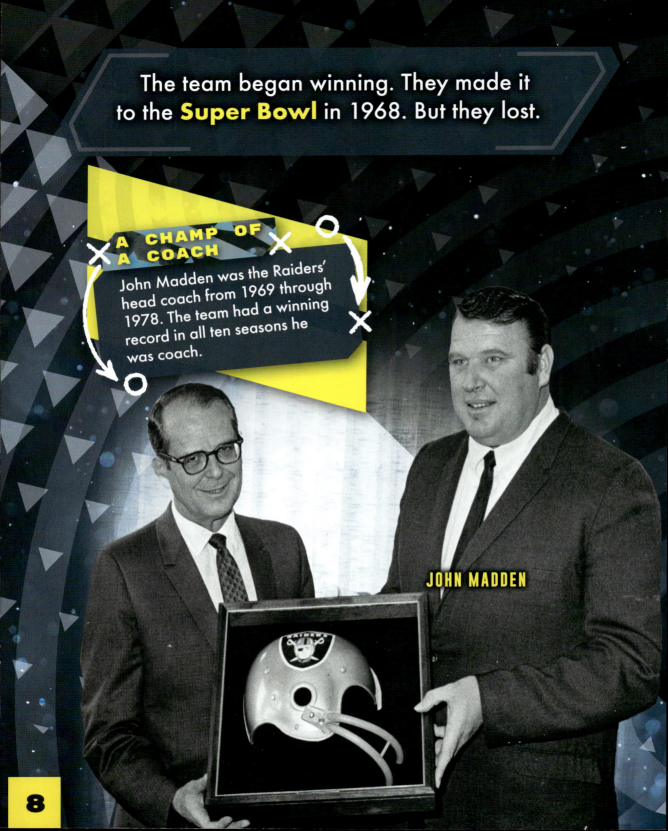

JOHN MADDEN

SUPER BOWL 11

In 1970, they joined the National Football League (NFL). They remained a strong team through the 1970s. In 1977, they won their first Super Bowl!

The Raiders won the Super Bowl again in 1981. The next year, the team moved from Oakland to Los Angeles, California.

TERRIFIC TEAMMATE

Cliff Branch was key to the Raiders' Super Bowl wins in the 1980s. He scored in both games!

CLIFF BRANCH

10

In 1984, the Raiders returned to the Super Bowl. They won 38–9!

The Raiders moved back to Oakland in 1995. The team played in the Super Bowl in 2003. But they lost.

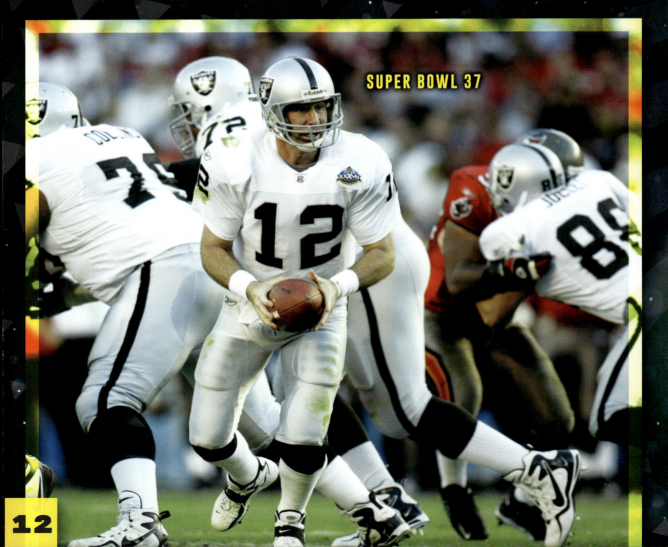

SUPER BOWL 37

The Raiders moved to Las Vegas, Nevada, in 2020. They had a winning record in their second season there.

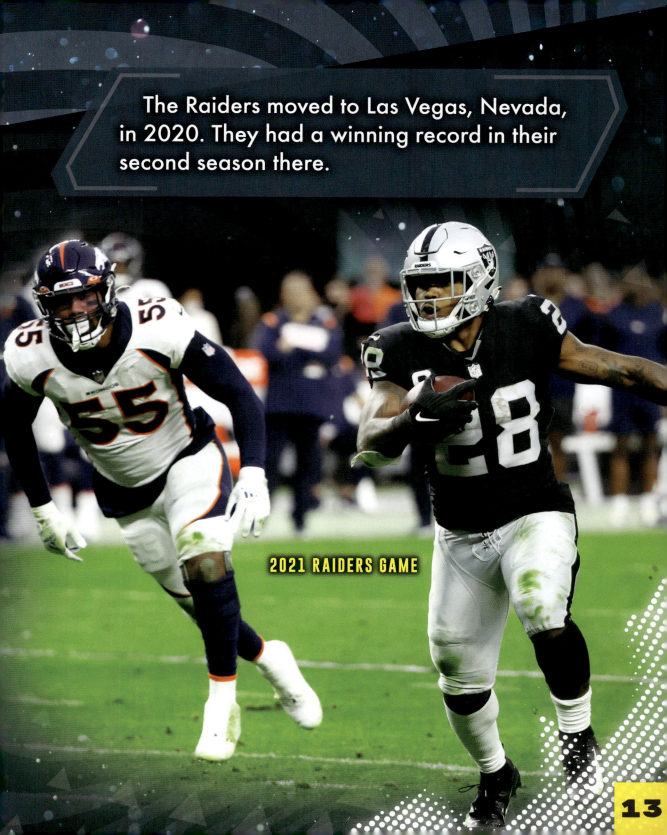

2021 RAIDERS GAME

13

THE RAIDERS TODAY

RAIDERS VS. CHIEFS

The Raiders play home games at Allegiant **Stadium**. It is in Las Vegas, Nevada.

The team plays in the AFC West **division**. Their main **rivals** are the Kansas City Chiefs, the Denver Broncos, and the Los Angeles Chargers.

SO MUCH STEEL

It took 28,000 tons (25,401 metric tons) of steel to build Allegiant Stadium. That is more than the Statue of Liberty!

LOCATION

ALLEGIANT STADIUM
Las Vegas, Nevada

15

GAME DAY!

Raider Rusher is the fun-loving team **mascot**. He high-fives fans on game days. Many fans dress in silver and black, the main team colors. Since 1974, "Autumn Wind" has been a Raiders theme song. It fires up fans during games.

RAIDER RUSHER

The Black Hole is a part of the Raiders' stadium. Extra loud fans often cheer from here. Many try to look scary. Some dress like pirates.

The Las Vegas Raiders fight to win all season long!

THE BLACK HOLE

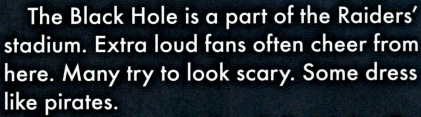

FAMOUS PLAYERS

63

GENE UPSHAW
Guard
Played 1967–1981

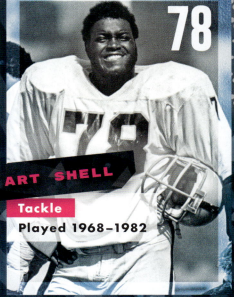

78

ART SHELL
Tackle
Played 1968–1982

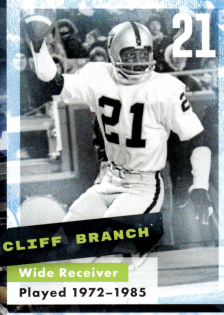

21

CLIFF BRANCH
Wide Receiver
Played 1972–1985

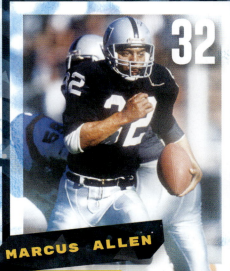

32

MARCUS ALLEN
Running Back
Played 1982–1992

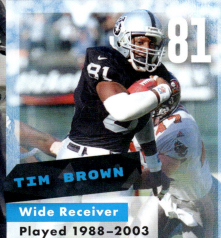

81

TIM BROWN
Wide Receiver
Played 1988–2003

19

LAS VEGAS RAIDERS FACTS

LOGO

JOINED THE NFL	1970 (AFL 1960-1969)
NICKNAME	The Silver and Black

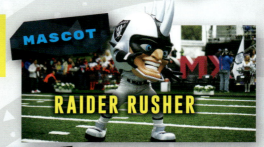
MASCOT: RAIDER RUSHER

CONFERENCE  American Football Conference (AFC)

COLORS

DIVISION | AFC West

 Denver Broncos    Kansas City Chiefs   Los Angeles Chargers

STADIUM

★ ALLEGIANT STADIUM ★
August 14, 2020

holds **65,000** people

20

🕐 TIMELINE

1960 The Raiders play their first season in the AFL

1977 The Raiders win Super Bowl 11

1982 The Raiders move to Los Angeles, California

1995 The Raiders return to Oakland

2020 The Raiders move to Las Vegas, Nevada

★ RECORDS ★

All-Time Passing Leader | **All-Time Rushing Leader** | **All-Time Receiving Leader** | **All-Time Scoring Leader**

Derek Carr — 35,222 yards

Marcus Allen — 8,545 yards

Tim Brown — 14,734 yards

Sebastian Janikowski — 1,799 points

GLOSSARY

division—a group of NFL teams from the same area that often play against each other; there are eight divisions in the NFL.

field goal—a score in football worth three points

first down—a gain of a total of 10 or more yards that allows a team to start a new series of downs; teams get four downs to gain 10 yards.

mascot—an animal or symbol that represents a sports team

playoffs—games played after the regular season is over; playoff games determine which teams play in the championship game.

rivals—long-standing opponents

running back—a player whose main job is to run with the ball

stadium—an arena where sports are played

Super Bowl—the annual championship game of the NFL

TO LEARN MORE

AT THE LIBRARY

Anderson, Josh. *Las Vegas Raiders*. Mankato, Minn.: The Child's World, 2022.

Goodman, Michael E. *Las Vegas Raiders*. Mankato, Minn.: Creative Education, 2023.

Kelley, K.C. *The Story of the Las Vegas Raiders*. Minneapolis, Minn.: Kaleidoscope, 2020.

ON THE WEB

FACTSURFER

Factsurfer.com gives you a safe, fun way to find more information.

1. Go to www.factsurfer.com.

2. Enter "Las Vegas Raiders" into the search box and click 🔍.

3. Select your book cover to see a list of related content.

INDEX

AFC West, 15, 20

Allegiant Stadium, 14, 15, 17, 18, 20

American Football League (AFL), 6, 20

Black Hole, 18

Branch, Cliff, 10

Carlson, Daniel, 5

colors, 16, 20

Davis, Al, 6, 7

famous players, 19

fans, 16, 18

history, 4, 5, 6, 7, 8, 9, 10, 11, 12, 13, 16

Jacobs, Josh, 4, 5

Las Vegas, Nevada, 13, 14, 15

Las Vegas Raiders facts, 20–21

Los Angeles, California, 10

Madden, John, 8

mascot, 16, 20

National Football League (NFL), 9, 20

Oakland, California, 6, 10, 12

playoffs, 5

positions, 5

records, 13, 21

rivals, 15

Super Bowl, 8, 9, 10, 11, 12

theme song, 16

timeline, 21

trophy case, 11

The images in this book are reproduced through the courtesy of: ASSOCIATED PRESS/ AP Images, cover (hero), p. 16; Kit Leong, cover (stadium); June Rivera/ Wikipedia, p. 3; Ethan Miller/ Getty, pp. 4-5, 13, 14, 18-19; Ric Tapia/ AP Images, p. 5; ROBERT KLEIN/ AP Images, p. 6; Ron Riesterer/ AP Images, pp. 6-7, 19 (Cliff Branch, Tim Brown); ZUMA Press Inc/ Alamy, p. 8; Focus On Sport/ Getty, p. 9; AP, AP Images, p. 10; Allen Kee/ AP Images, p. 12; Kirby Lee/ AP Images, p. 15; NFL/ Wikipedia, p. 15 (Raiders logo), 20 (Raiders logo, Broncos logo, Chiefs logo, Chargers logo, AFC logo); Aaron M. Sprecher/ AP Images, pp. 16-17; MESSA/ AP Images, p. 19 (Gene Upshaw); GOLUA/ AP Images p. 19 (Art Shell); Peter Brouillet/ Getty, p. 19 (Marcus Allen); Hector Vivas/ Getty, p. 20 (mascot); Katherine Welles, p. 20 (stadium); San Francisco Chronicle/ AP Images, p. 21 (1960); Tony Tomsic, p. 21 (1977); Peter Read Miller/ AP Images, p. 21 (1982, Marcus Allen); George Rose/ Getty, p. 21 (1995); LEEKI/ AP Images, p. 21 (2020); TAPIR/ AP Images, p. 21 (Derek Carr); TROTG/ AP Images, p. 21 (Tim Brown); Al GOLUB/ AP Images, p. 21 (Sebastian Janikowski); Jamie Lamor Thompson, p. 23.